In My Neighborhood

POLICE OFFICERS

First U.S. edition 1999
Text copyright © 1992 by Paulette Bourgeois
Illustrations copyright © 1992 by Kim LaFave

With thanks to the Metropolitan Toronto Police and to Judge Donna Hackett – P.B.

With thanks to the RCMP Sechelt Detachment and for my dad, PC 260 LaFave (Ret.) – K.L.

Published in Canada by
Kids Can Press Ltd.
29 Birch Avenue
Toronto, ON M4V 1E2

Published in the U.S. by
Kids Can Press Ltd.
85 River Rock Drive, Suite 202
Buffalo, NY 14207

Designed by N.R. Jackson
Typeset by Cybergraphics Co. Inc.
Printed in Hong Kong by Sheck Wah Tong Printing Press Limited

US 99 0 9 8 7 6 5 4 3 2 1

Canadian Cataloguing in Publication Data

Bourgeois, Paulette
Police officers

(In my neighborhood)
ISBN 1-55074-502-6

1. Police -- United States -- Juvenile literature. I.
LaFave, Kim.
II. Series: Bourgeois, Paulette. In my neighborhood.

HV8138.B595 1998   j363.2'0973   C98-931964-4

In My Neighborhood

POLICE OFFICERS

Paulette Bourgeois
Kim LaFave

KIDS CAN PRESS

Everybody is asleep.
"Clank, clang, clatter, bang!"
Natalie hears the commotion and she's
worried. Somebody has been stealing bicycles
in the neighborhood. Maybe the thieves are
in her garage! Natalie creeps into her parents'
room and whispers, "Call the police."

Natalie's mother reaches for the phone —
the police number is written clearly nearby.
When the phone is answered, she says, "We
think somebody is trying to break in. Our
name is Best. We live at 123 Main Street.
The closest intersection is Main and South streets."

"Don't worry," she tells Natalie. "The police
will be right here."

As soon as the police dispatcher gets the call, a message is sent to the computer or radio inside the patrol car closest to the Bests' house.

Usually, the officers work in pairs. As soon as they hear the message, the officers signal to the dispatcher that they are on the way. In some emergencies, lots of police cars are sent. The officers do not use their siren this time — they want to arrive quietly and catch the thieves in action.

The officers use their flashlights to search the
neighborhood. A garbage can has been
knocked over but there is no sign that somebody has tried to break open doors or windows.
They jot in their notebooks and keep on looking.

"All quiet now," they tell the Best family.
"There have been a lot of bicycle thefts around
here. Do you have a good lock on your
bike?" they ask. Natalie nods. "And I registered
my bicycle with the police department.
You have the make, the color and the
registration number in your computer," she says.

"That's smart!" say the officers.
"Sometimes we find lost or
stolen bicycles and we don't
know who owns them."

On the way to school, Natalie notices something suspicious. There is a big blue van parked behind an abandoned building. She writes the license plate number in her notebook and tells the principal when she gets to school. The principal calls the police.

The officers drive slowly by the schoolyard. At
the bike rack, they see two men look around
nervously and then, in a flash, slice through
a bicycle lock with a small saw.

Just as they are about to
ride off, the police officers
tell them they are under
arrest for stealing, and they
are going for a different ride
— to the police station.

At the station, the men are taken to a room to be questioned by police detectives. The men can ask for a lawyer to be present. The police officers who made the arrest still have work to do. They look in the back of the blue van — there are 15 bicycles inside!

The men are let go until their trial in a courtroom. In court, a lawyer for the accused men and a lawyer for the government, who is called a District Attorney, will ask the police officers questions about what they saw. It will be the judge's job to decide if the men are guilty of stealing bicycles and, if they are, to decide on a punishment.

Later that night, Natalie hears "Clank, clang, clatter, bang!"

"The bike thieves are back!" she calls to her parents. "Call the police!"

The officers arrive within seconds. They move quickly and quietly through the dark. They shine their flashlights into the alley.

"I've caught the masked robbers," says the officer. "But I think we'll let them go with a warning."

A police officer has to be prepared for anything.

All police officers are ready to help people who
are lost, hurt or afraid. They are your friends.
The police make sure people obey the law.
And there are many different kinds of police
work. Some officers teach children to be safe.

Some officers control the crowds at concerts and sports events.

Some officers investigate crimes and traffic accidents.

There are many different kinds of police. All villages, towns and cities have a police department. Large cities are too big for just one police building, so the city is set up with many offices, or police precincts. Sometimes a precinct in one section of a city will help a precinct in another section solve crimes.

Police who wear uniforms patrol the neighborhood by car, walk on foot, ride a horse or even patrol by bicycle.

Sometimes police may fool a criminal by wearing regular street clothes and pretending they are not police officers. This form of police work is called "undercover." A criminal might commit a crime while an undercover officer looks on. An undercover officer may foil a bank robbery while pretending to be a bank customer!

The Federal Bureau of Investigation, or FBI, works all across America. An FBI agent may have to conduct an investigation through many different states in order to solve a crime.

Some police officers walk in the neighborhood and get to know all the people in their community. But the police get around in lots of different ways:

in a van

in a helicopter

on a motorcyle

in a boat

on a bicycle

in a patrol car.

Police officers are physically fit. They are not too short and not too tall. They must have good eyesight. Police officers have revolvers but they hope they never have to use them.

Sometimes officers wear bulletproof vests. They carry notebooks and handcuffs and wear a belt with a nightstick and a flashlight.

Remember to Stay Alert and
Stay Safe

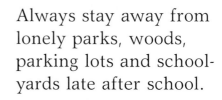

Always stick with the same route for
going to and from school, playgrounds
and friends' homes. Make sure
your parents know the routes
you take. Check the route
over with a parent for
possible unsafe places.

Always stay away from
lonely parks, woods,
parking lots and school-
yards late after school.

Always go places with
buddies and make sure your
parents know where you are at
all times. Keep your friends'
addresses and phone
numbers by your phone.

Always say "No" if anybody
invites you alone into his or
her home or car — even if
you're with friends.

Always tell your parent or an adult you trust if something has happened that bothers you, even if it is about somebody your family knows well and likes. It's not your fault if somebody acts in a way that makes you uncomfortable. You don't have to keep it a secret no matter what anyone says.

Always keep the door closed and locked when you are home alone.

Always pretend you've got grown-up company if you're home alone.

Always have a family password. Adults who want you to stay with them, or go somewhere with them, must know the password.

Always refuse to go anywhere with a stranger or somebody who makes you feel uncomfortable — no matter what they say to you. Most people are helpful and kind, but some people are mean. They might try to trick you by offering you something nice such as a kitten, a puppy, a toy or an ice cream. They might try to trick you by telling you that something is wrong with your parents. They might even trick you by telling you that you are going to be on a television show or made famous if you go with them.

Never go anywhere with a stranger.

DATE			